THE LITTLE BOOK OF
Emmerdale

G000055169

Thanks to Helen,
as fine a li'l archivist as
ever bit a biscuit.

THE LITTLE BOOK OF
Emmerdale

EDITED AND WRITTEN BY FINTAN OHIGGINS

GRANADA

Emmerdale is a Granada Television Production

First published by Granada Media, 2002
An imprint of Andre Deutsch, Ltd
20 Mortimer Street
London
W1T 3JW

A catalogue record of this book is available from the
British Library.

ISBN 0 233 05085 X

Managing Art Director: Jeremy Southgate

Printed and bound in Singapore

PRODUCER'S FOREWORD

Looking over *The Little Book of Emmerdale*, it's amazing to think how many characters and how many stories have been told in this little village over the last thirty years. The seventy-odd characters included here represent just a fraction of more than seven hundred faces which have graced the village.

Of course there's no way to do justice to all of them, but I hope this small selection will remind you of the favourite personalities you have enjoyed

over the years – and give you
a taste of the treats in store for the
future.

It goes without saying that enormous
gratitude is due to Kevin Laffan,
creator of *Emmerdale Farm*, without
whom none of these characters could
ever have existed, and whose
inspiration has been an inspiration to
everybody connected with the show
down through the years.

Steve Frost
Emmerdale Producer
June 2002

THE ORIGINAL FAMILY

Kevin Laffan's original ITV serial, *Emmerdale Farm*, focused on the trials of one family, and the members of the extended Sugden clan continued to be the focus and mainstay of the show for years to come.

Emmerdale

JACK SUGDEN
FIRST APPEARANCE: 1972
BORN: 28 NOVEMBER 1947

There have always been Sugdens on *Emmerdale Farm*, and novelist, playboy and jailbird Jack is the current incumbent. No longer master of his land (he was forced to sell up after a long financial struggle), Jack nevertheless represents the history and heritage of *Emmerdale*.

Emmerdale

The show began with his return to claim his inheritance on his father's death and has followed his triumphs and tragedies – his struggles with brother Joe and long-lost son Jackie Merrick – for thirty years.

Emmerdale

Jack's been married twice, most recently to Victoria's mother Sarah who burned to death while in the process of leaving her teenage lover Richie Carter. Jack's also been linked romantically to his step-niece, Rachel Hughes, and to Diane Blackstock.

Emmerdale

Nowadays he's estate manager on Home Farm and is proud to see his legacy carried on by adopted son Andy, whose rivalry with son Robert seems to echo Jack's own troubles with Joe.

Emmerdale

JOE SUGDEN
FIRST APPEARANCE: 1972
BORN: 1949

Heart-throb Joe was one of the longest-serving cast members, he appeared in the show for 22 years. Joe was twice married and had a long string of romances, making him a favourite until his tragic death in a car crash in 1995.

Emmerdale

ANNIE SUGDEN
FIRST APPEARANCE: 1972
BORN: 1920

Mother of Jack, Joe and Peggy, Annie
was a proper earth mother figure,
demanding, capable and strongly
moral. The backbone of the village for
many years, she left for Spain after
marrying Leonard Kempinski in 1992.
After his death, Annie fittingly married
Amos Brearly who was also one of
Emmerdale Farm's original characters.

MATT SKILBECK
FIRST APPEARANCE: 1972
BORN: ?

Married to Peggy, Matt was brother-in-law to Joe and Jack. After Peggy's death, Matt married Dolly Acaster, but the marriage ended and in 1989, Matt left the village where he had been a familiar face for so many years.

PEGGY SKILBECK
FIRST APPEARANCE: 1972
BORN; ?

Joe and Jack's sister, she was more ambitious than her husband Matt and aggrieved by Jack's being bequeathed *Emmerdale Farm*. She died tragically of a brain haemorrhage in 1973.

Emmerdale

SAM PEARSON
FIRST APPEARANCE: 1972
BORN: 1896

Father of Annie, and a hardworking countryman, Sam was a repository of wisdom. His chief occupations were smoking his pipe and dispensing canny observations on the nature of the world.

Emmerdale

AMOS BREARLY AND HENRY WILKS
FIRST APPEARANCE: 1972
BORN: 1920 AND 1921

Among the longest-serving and best-loved pairings in soap, Amos and Mr Wilks had an enduring, touching and incomprehensible working partnership that lasted until 1991. Amos was a stick-in-the-mud who disapproved of women and the modern world; Mr Wilks was a retired wool-merchant from Bradford.

Emmerdale

Though personally close, Amos and Mr Wilks's relationship was formal; the most demonstrative either of them became was on Amos's departure from the Woolpack after 43 years when he called Mr Wilks by his Christian name for the first time. (see pg 126)

Emmerdale

SETH ARMSTRONG
FIRST APPEARANCE: 1978
BORN: 26 NOVEMBER 1926
(PROBABLY)

Poacher-turned-gamekeeper-turned-general layabout, Seth is *Emmerdale*'s longest-serving character and the Woolpack's most valuable customer. He was devastated after the death of wife Meg, but found love with long-lost childhood sweetheart Betty Eagleton.

Emmerdale

Seth now spends his time gambling and dispensing wisdom from his corner of the bar. When not engaged in his valuable boozing work, Seth devotes his spare time to maintaining his website and avoiding Betty's nagging.

Emmerdale

JACKIE MERRICK
FIRST APPEARANCE: 1980
BORN: ?

Hapless Jackie Merrick had to come to terms with the news that his real father was Jack Sugden. He was killed in a hunting accident and had the distinction of giving Kathy Glover/ Tate/ Merrick/ Bates her first taste of widowhood.

Emmerdale

ALAN TURNER
FIRST APPEARANCE: 1982
BORN: 1935

As manager of Home Farm estate, Turner was a snob, a bully and a martinet, in spite of an unfortunate tendency to fall for prostitutes and (worse) barmaids. He has mellowed in his old age and given up life in the Woolpack. He now spends his time running the B&B and indulging wayward granddaughter Tricia Stokes.

Emmerdale

KATHY GLOVER (NÉE BATES, FORMERLY TATE, FORMERLY MERRICK)
FIRST APPEARANCE: 1985
BORN: 1967

Perky blonde Kathy was actually the Black Widow of Emmerdale. She survived two husbands – Jackie Merrick and Dave Glover and left one (Chris Tate) with a permanent disability. Despite these and other misfortunes – one miscarriage, one defeated tug-of-love over niece Alice Bates, one attempted kidnap by psycho Graham Clark – Kathy always came up smiling.

Emmerdale

Her blonde hair, pretty smile and indefatigable spirit lured many men to misery. The last was stud farm manager Andrew Fraser. He supported her through her battle with Elsa over Alice, and was left broken-hearted when she ran off to Australia.

As well as breaking hearts and surviving husbands, Kathy also worked as a shepherdess, stable hand and poultry assistant.

Emmerdale

She ran tea-rooms, a diner and a restaurant and managed to hold the Sugden family together when Jack was in prison. Perhaps most unusual was her musical success – she achieved a local hit as Kathy Merrick and the Christopher Tate Quartet with 'Just This Side of Love', written by Chris in a rare sensitive moment.

Emmerdale

ROBERT SUGDEN
FIRST APPEARANCE 1986
BORN 1986

Jack Sugden's natural son, Robert has had the misfortune to lose not one but two mothers. The death of Sarah by fire left him devastated and fuelled his resentment of adoptive brother Andy. Robert is clever and ambitious and although he has no interest in farming, he is bitter about Andy's perceived supplanting of him in Jack's affections.

Emmerdale

ERIC AND GLORIA POLLARD
ERIC'S FIRST APPEARANCE: 1986
BORN: 1945
GLORIA'S FIRST APPEARANCE: 2000
BORN: 1953

Dour, scheming, grasping and dishonest, Emmerdale's mayor is justly loathed throughout Emmerdale and its environs. Pollard has been – among other things – a professional antiques dealer and wine bar proprietor, but he now spends his time running his tat factory and plotting with Gloria to swindle and manipulate his way into Parliament.

Emmerdale

Gloria 'Lady Macbeth' Pollard (formerly Weaver) arrived in 2000 and is the latest and most successful in a line of Mrs Pollards. Dee Dee the Filipina mail-order bride broke Pollard's black heart when she abandoned him. Previous wife Elizabeth didn't have the chance to run away. She died in mysterious circumstances on the night of the plane crash. No case was ever brought against evil Eric, but those who know him know he is not above the odd discreetly-executed murder…

Emmerdale

RACHEL TATE (NÉE HUGHES)
FIRST APPEARANCE: 1988
BORN: 1971

As sweet-natured and popular as Kathy Glover/ Tate/ Merrick/ Bates, Rachel was marginally less destructive. She was nevertheless responsible for destroying a fair few lives. She was seduced by married man Pete Whiteley and this set a pattern for her future career as a homebreaker.

Emmerdale

She was instrumental in the break-up of best friend Kathy Glover/ Tate/ Merrick/ Bates's marriage to Chris Tate and her step-uncle Jack Sugden's marriage to Sarah Connolly.

Emmerdale

Always well meaning, Rachel's fatal flaw was to fall for unsuitable men, and none could have been more unsuitable than psycho Graham Clark, who pushed her off a cliff to a horrible death.

Emmerdale

KIM AND FRANK TATE
FIRST APPEARANCE: 1989
BORN: 1959 AND 1937

Providing a heady mix of power, money, sex and glamour, Frank and Kim were the very essence of a high-powered soap couple.

Emmerdale

Frank, who took over Home farm in 1990, was a hardnosed businessman; tough and ruthless himself, but an alcoholic and in thrall to the evil Kim. He tried to have the Dingles evicted from their property and was rumoured to have killed his first wife. But although he threw Kim out and horsewhipped her lover Neil Kincaid, Frank and Kim were reunited after the plane crash.

Emmerdale

Kim was scheming, manipulative, sexy and ruthless. She broke the heart of handsome but hapless Dave Glover and was partly responsible for his death by burning.

Emmerdale

During her two marriages to Frank, she pursued a course of deceit, infidelity, manipulation and ruthless conniving. Her coldhearted bitchery was exemplified when she coolly watched Frank die and her exit in a helicopter, leaving hated stepson Chris crawling on the ground, has passed into legend.

Emmerdale

CHRIS AND ZOE TATE
FIRST APPEARANCE: 1989
BORN: 1963 AND 1968

This millionaire brother-sister team have one of *Emmerdale*'s odder relationships. Among other things, they have between them killed their psychotic half-brother and shared a girlfriend (they are very close).

Emmerdale

Although wives and lovers have come and gone (Kathy, Rachel, Kelly for him; Emma Nightingale and Frankie Smith for her), their principle relationship is with each other.

Emmerdale

The plane crash left Chris without the use of his legs but his real disability is his struggle to live up to dead father Frank. Chris only relates to people on business terms – his only friend is Terry, and he's on a good salary. Chris found a perverse closeness with half-brother Liam, but the unfortunate circumstance of being held hostage in a cellar at the time meant that the relationship was doomed.

Emmerdale

Zoe is suspected to be schizophrenic. It's the latest in a line of traumas which include her murder of Liam and her struggle to come out as a lesbian (Archie Brooks had the dubious honour of confirming Zoe in her homosexuality).

Chris and Zoe are business partners in Tate Haulage, but their principle joint venture is bringing up Joseph, Chris's son by dead wife Rachel.

Emmerdale

VIV HOPE (FORMERLY WINDSOR, FORMERLY DAWSON)
FIRST APPEARANCE: 1993
BORN: 1956

Emmerdale's postmistress would be the first to admit that she keeps a lively interest in village affairs. However, she might be more resistant to the more accurate title of badly-dressed spreader of malicious gossip. Viv's gift for criticising others is matched only by her enormous capacity for self-delusion.

Emmerdale

Her grandiose schemes have included a modelling career, standing for Parliament and seducing young Richie Carter. All failed.

Viv's suffered her share of tragedy – she's a widow twice over – and she seemed destined to a life of loneliness until hosiery salesman Bob Hope brought the light of love to her life.

Emmerdale

SCOTT AND DONNA WINDSOR
FIRST APPEARANCE: 1993
BORN: 1980 AND 1986

Any children of Viv Hope's were bound to be in for a rough time. Scott's father was killed by a marksman at Home Farm and Donna's was killed in a Post Office raid. Scott's affair with step-sister Kelly nearly tore apart the family.

Emmerdale

Scott seemed to be settled into a stable relationship with Chloe Atkinson, but it appears that crime is in the genes, and his involvement with Ray Mullan's car-ringing broke up the relationship. While Donna pursues her modelling career, Scott's return to his role of womanising bad boy seems inevitable.

Emmerdale

KELLY WINDSOR
FIRST APPEARANCE: 1993
BORN: 1980

Daughter of Vic and Viv's step-daughter, Kelly was a minx. She seduced her teacher, slept with (among others) her sister-in-law Linda's husband Biff, and her *own* step-brother Scott. Being Viv's step-daughter was never an easy job, but when Kelly tried to seduce Viv's new beau Bob in an attempt to split them up, Viv saw red and Kelly left the village – alone and in ignominy.

BIFF FOWLER
FIRST APPEARANCE: 1994
BORN: 1976

Good-looking chauffeur Biff had an unhappy addiction to doomed romances. His first wife Linda (née Glover) died tragically in a car-crash and he was heartbroken when new love Lady Tara Oakwell went ahead with her wedding to Lord Michael Thornfield. Biff was subsequently engaged to Kathy Glover/ Tate/ Merrick/ Bates, but left her at the altar and disappeared from the village forever.

Emmerdale

BETTY EAGLETON
FIRST APPEARANCE: 1994
BORN: 1934

Former Tiller girl, part-time cleaner, full-time gossip and internet superstar, Betty's keen ear and sharp tongue make her a force to be reckoned with in the village. Along with cronies Viv and Edna, Betty is the engine that powers the Emmerdale gossip machine.

Emmerdale

But if she's curious, she's never malicious and never slow to offer a shoulder to cry on and is the constant scourge and comfort of her live-in lover, Emmerdale's senior resident Seth Armstrong.

Emmerdale

THE GLOVERS
FIRST APPEARANCE: 1994
BORN: NED 1947; JAN 1950;
ROY: 1980; DAVE 1973;
LINDA 1978

Roy Glover was one of life's losers.
Not only did his wife, Kelly sleep with
her step-brother Scott, but his mother Jan
went mad, his father Ned disowned him
and his sister Linda died in a car crash.

Poor Dave didn't fare much better. He gave his heart to the heartless Kim Tate and was killed in his heroic attempt to rescue their baby James from a fire. Dave also had the misfortune to marry Kathy Tate/ Merrick/ Bates. Enough said.

Emmerdale

ZAK DINGLE
FIRST APPEARANCE: 1994
BORN: 1952

Pig magnate, metallurgical entrepreneur and former prize-fighter, Zak is the formidable head of the Dingle clan. Proud and headstrong, he is fiercely protective of his family's pride, and his family is extensive and troublesome. Zak's chief profession is as a skiver, and he has skived successfully in the various demanding fields of rubbish-collecting and, perhaps surprisingly, recycling.

Emmerdale

Zak's fierce devotion to his family and his status has received some tragic blows. He has witnessed the death of two sons, Ben and Butch, whose tragic death in the bus crash led to a violent feud with the powerful Tates.

Emmerdale

Zak was also stunned by the revelation that his wicked nephew Cain is really his son. Throughout all this and his battle with testicular cancer, he has been supported by his second wife Lisa, mother of Belle and occasional stepmother to Sam.

Emmerdale

FRANCIS 'BUTCH' DINGLE
FIRST APPEARANCE: 1994
BORN: 1972

Butch was a gentle-hearted thug, Zak's co-conspirator and favourite son. A man of simple pleasures (boozing, thieving) and strong emotions, he hated Luke McAllister whom he blamed for the death of his brother Ben, but loved his rat Jessica (platonically), his cousin Mandy (hopelessly), the nanny Sophie (dangerously – he began stalking her and had to be told off by Zak).

Emmerdale

His last and greatest love was Emily
Wylie whom he loved utterly and
romantically. Butch and Emily were
married as he lay dying from injuries
sustained in the bus crash.

Emmerdale

MANDY DINGLE
FIRST APPEARANCE: 1995
BORN: 1977

Mandy was a bruiser, a troublemaker and a fast-food entrepreneur. She was stalwart in the Dingles' stand to resist eviction. She pursued her hopeless crush on Dave Glover and avoided the attentions of her cousin Butch (although she did end up briefly marrying him). She was wooed and won by Paddy Kirk in a fairytale romance, but broke his heart when she had an affair with her father's carer.

SAM DINGLE
FIRST APPEARANCE: 1994
BORN: 1977

Sam likes pigs and fishing. Zak's youngest child by Nellie and his stalwart sidekick, it would be unkind to describe Sam as a village idiot.

Emmerdale

TERRY WOODS
FIRST APPEARANCE: 1995
BORN: 1957

Stalwart best mate, all-round good guy and perpetual loser, Terry lives a life of frustration. Having lost the Woolpack and wife Britt, the former rugby star now ekes his living as dogsbody-cum-confidant to surly Chris Tate. Terry has a taste for unattainable women, and although he's managed to bed a few – including Tricia who slept with him out of sympathy – he always ends up alone.

Emmerdale

**ANDY SUGDEN
FIRST APPEARANCE: 1996
BORN: 1986**

Adopted by Jack and Sarah Sugden, Andy is determined to follow in the footsteps of Emmerdale Farm's sturdiest son. Although he is understandably less keen to emulate Sarah, whom he accidentally burned to death in Jack's barn. Jack went to jail for this.

Emmerdale

Andy had a rough childhood – his father, Billy Hopwood, was responsible for Vic Windsor's death in the Post Office raid. Billy is now in jail for this. It's tough work being Andy Sugden's father.

But in spite of his chequered past – and his record two fathers' imprisonments – Andy has a heart of gold.

Emmerdale

He's only ever wanted to be loved and seems to have found the real thing with Katie Addyman – although the course of their true love has run far from smoothly, faced as they are with their fathers' implacable hostility, and their drastic decision to have a baby. Well, love conquers all, they say, so let's hope it can triumph for Andy – without another hideous death if possible.

LISA DINGLE
FIRST APPEARANCE: 1996
BORN: 1956

Formerly married to no-good Barry Clegg, Lisa is now consort to Zak, and the power behind the Dingle throne. Mother to Belle and stepmother to Sam, Lisa – for all Zak's posturing and bluster – is the lynchpin of the Dingle household, although her relationship with Cain is strained at best.

Emmerdale

MARLON DINGLE
FIRST APPEARANCE: 1996
BORN: 1974

Woolpack chef Marlon fancies himself as the artistic Dingle, but his ambition sometimes outstretches his abilities. His plans for *Chez Marlon* – Emmerdale's centre of *haute cuisine* – ended in failure and his self-image as a lady-killing wide-boy got a kick in the teeth from reality.

Emmerdale

In fact Marlon's neurotic artistic temperament makes him a gooey romantic, and in spite of a brief slip-up with locum vet Rhona Goskirk, he is utterly devoted to his beloved fiancée Tricia Stokes (formerly – and very complicatedly – Fisher).

Emmerdale

ASHLEY THOMAS
FIRST APPEARANCE: 1996
BORN: 1961

Wily man of God and much-needed conscience to the village, Ashley's world was turned upside down when he met Bernice Blackstock. He couldn't believe his luck when he wooed and finally won her – and he was right. Having been abandoned by the love of his life, Ashley struggles to bury himself in parish business and to raise his beloved daughter Gabrielle.

Emmerdale

PADDY KIRK
FIRST APPEARANCE: 1997
BORN: 1969

Mild-mannered vet Paddy Kirk's fairytale romance with Mandy Dingle turned sour when she had an affair with her father's carer. He has since found love with fellow honorary Dingle, Emily. They are now interminably engaged, but with a marriage apiece behind them, when they will marry is anyone's guess. His gentle nature and troublesome conscience can make him susceptible to bullying or manipulation. It's no wonder he was a perfect Dingle in-law.

Emmerdale

LADY TARA THORNFIELD
(FORMERLY OAKWELL, NÉE
COCKBURN)
FIRST APPEARANCE: 1997
BORN: 1974

Tara's tendency to fall for men from the lower orders clashed with her desperate addiction to social-climbing. She broke Biff Fowler's heart when she chose to marry Lord Michael Thornfield over him. She tore the Reynolds family apart when she embarked on a torrid affair with haulage boss Sean. Sean loathed Tara but couldn't stay away, and she enjoyed tormenting her.

Sean managed to end the affair but too late to stop his family from being destroyed. With the closure of the stud farm, which she co-owned with Chris and Zoe Tate, Tara became restless. She left Emmerdale with Sean, having patched things up in an unlikely way, and set out on a new life – trying to make a go of things with her bit of rough.

GRAHAM CLARK
FIRST APPEARANCE: 1998
BORN: 1971

Charming, yes, and handsome,
certainly, Graham Clark was
unfortunately also psychotic. This was
apparent to most people pretty quickly.
Sadly Rachel Tate only learned this
unhappy truth when Graham pushed
her off a cliff to meet a grisly death.

TRICIA STOKES
FIRST APPEARANCE: 1998
BORN: 1976

Alan Turner's granddaughter is as unlike her grandfather as colourful schoolyard chalks to a grand old Stilton. Where he's pompous and sage, the Woolpack's favourite barmaid is bubbly and maybe a little bit dizzy.

Emmerdale

She's been unlucky in love before – with a tendency to run away when things get rough, and to occasionally marry the odd visa-seeking Australian homosexual – but is now happily engaged to chef Marlon Dingle.

BERNICE THOMAS (NÉE BLACKSTOCK)
FIRST APPEARANCE: 1998
BORN: 1968

Bubbly barmaid Bernice brightened the Woolpack when she arrived as a temporary barmaid in 1998. Her ambition betrayed by her scattiness, she had the embarrassment to be engaged *twice* to two distinct and separate gay men.

And just when she thought she had found true love with vicar Ashley Thomas, it turned out to be not what she wanted at all. She threw it all away for a fling with her sister's fiancé Carlos Diaz, and abandoned Ashley and daughter Gabrielle to work on a Mediterranean cruise ship.

Emmerdale

THE REYNOLDS FAMILY
FIRST APPEARANCE: 1999
BORN: ANGIE 1965;
SEAN 1964; MARC 1984;
OLLIE 1985

Trucker Sean and copper Angie, childhood sweethearts, were a happy couple of twenty years' standing – before they arrived in Emmerdale. It proved to be an unwise decision, as Sean's enthralment to the bewitching Lady Tara split the family apart.

Emmerdale

Angie's explosively torrid affair with Cain Dingle finished off the job, especially when Cain revealed he'd slept with Sean's and Angie's feisty teenage daughter Ollie. If this wasn't bad enough, studious brother Marc was convicted of killing their head teacher. Somehow only cheery granddad, Edna's sidekick Len, seems to have anything to smile about. God knows what.

EMILY DINGLE
FIRST APPEARANCE: 1999
BORN: 1978

Quiet, intelligent, fiercely moral, Emily Dingle is undeniably an unusual figure in Emmerdale. She was brought up in isolation by her domineering father, but found love with Butch Dingle, to whom she was married on his deathbed.

Emily is now happily engaged to Paddy Kirk and works in the Post Office where she fulfils the crucial role of conscience, confidante and dogsbody to Viv Hope.

Emmerdale

DIANE BLACKSTOCK
FIRST APPEARANCE: 1999
BORN: 1947

Feisty barmaid Diane is a sixteen-year-old trapped in a fifty-five-year-old's body. She moved to the village to be with her daughter Bernice and her quick wit soon made her a favourite with the villagers. Diane's life previously had been carefree and irresponsible, but as Bernice lurched from crisis to crisis, Diane found herself rising to the task of supporting her daughter.

Emmerdale

Her own life has not been free of drama. She embarked on an affair with Alan Turner, but broke his heart when she fell in love with Jack Sugden. Jack rejected her when she suspected him of killing his wife Sarah and accidentally slept with her former husband Rodney. Since then she has had to endure the joyful trauma of becoming grandmother to Gabrielle and the heartache of Bernice's leaving Emmerdale.

Her burgeoning love affair with builder Jerry 'Mack' Mackinley was scuppered by an ill-timed mid-life crisis, and once again, Diane is on her own. She's a trooper, though, Diane, the voice of the Woolpack and the heart of the village. She can cope with whatever life has to throw at her: after all, she's still young...

CHARITY TATE (NÉE DINGLE)
FIRST APPEARANCE: 2000
BORN: 1978

Not long ago she was a prostitute working the streets of Leeds, but Charity Tate is now proud to be the lady of the manor at Home Farm. Her rise from the poverty of the Dingles to the opulence of the Tates has shown her to be tough and smart.

Emmerdale

Instigating a lesbian affair with her millionaire boyfriend's (now husband's) sister was maybe not such a smart move, but Charity's shrewdness (not to mention her other considerable attributes) assured that she came out on top – even managing to end the Tate-Dingle feud.

CAIN DINGLE
FIRST APPEARANCE: 2000
BORN: 1974

Thug, psycho, Madchester throwback, bad boy Cain brings an element of sexy danger to the Dingle household. A career criminal and emotional sadist, behind Cain's bravado and swagger is a lost and unloved child.

Emmerdale

Cain was brought up by his mother Faith and Zak's useless brother Shadrach, but has struggled to find his role in the Dingle family after learning that Zak is his real father. Suspicious of emotion, he has allowed himself to fall in love once – and the ensuing affair with Angie Reynolds destroyed her family and left Cain scarred forever.

Emmerdale

OTHER DINGLES

The Dingle clan of itinerant horse dealers, antiques dealers, lumberjacks, thieves and poets (yes) is extensive and as yet uncatalogued.

Emmerdale

Among those confirmed to exist are: Shadrach, Albert, Esra, Jed (deceased), Charlton, Peg, Marilyn and Elvis. More contentious is the existence of, Orbison, Ferdinand, Vercingetorix Dingle. Last but by no means least, we must never forget Tina Dingle, Zac's wayward daughter, who dumped Luke McAllister at the altar and ran away to university.

Emmerdale

If she was an animal she'd be a dragon; if she was a weapon she'd be a battle-axe; there's definitely something mediaeval about the most prominent member of Emmerdale's parish council. Mind you if they still burned witches, it's hard to say if Edna would be the first victim or the one responsible for biccies and orange squash afterwards.

In spite of her harsh tongue, though, Edna has a soft side. Her heart was broken after the death of her long-time companion, Batley and she provided great comfort to Bernice after her miscarriage. Nonetheless it's her interfering, small-minded, judgemental side that has most endeared her to her friends.

Emmerdale

BOB HOPE
FIRST APPEARANCE: 2000
BORN: ?

With a smile, a song and a nifty line in hosiery, travelling salesman Bob crashed into Emmerdale and Viv Hope's life like a gift from above. Although some doubted his honesty at first, Mr Tickles has won over all doubters with his winning ways and his overpowering (if incomprehensible) love for his fourth wife Viv.

Emmerdale

RODNEY BLACKSTOCK
FIRST APPEARANCE: 2000
BORN: 1949

Aging playboy, entrepreneur and wanderer, Rodney is Bernice's long-lost father and Diane's misplaced ex. Rodney wheeled into town for Bernice's wedding and has been in the B&B ever since. While Rodney has dabbled in business with Chris Tate and Ray Mullan, his chief occupation is making Diane very angry indeed. Although he had a brief fling with Louise and has bedded Diane for old time's sake, Rodney's most important relationship is with his impossible daughter Nicola.

Emmerdale

NICOLA BLACKSTOCK.
FIRST APPEARANCE: 2001
BORN 1978

She came in like champagne, sweet and frothy, but the bubble burst for daddy's girl Nicola when she discovered her fiancé Carlos was having an affair with her beloved half-sister Bernice. Things have soured since then and Nicola's manipulative scheming has made her enemies all over Emmerdale. Only her one friend, Emily, seems willing to forgive her foibles… and she can always wrap Rodney around her little finger.

Emmerdale

THE DAGGERTS
FIRST APPEARANCE: 2001
BORN: CYNTHIA 1967;
LATISHA 1983; DANNY 1985;
KIRK 2001

Cynthia and teenage son Danny came from Bradford to Emmerdale to find a peaceful life. They came to the wrong place. They were joined soon after by Latisha, whose baby Kirk was born on her arrival in the village. Since their arrival, the Daggerts have rubbed a lot of people up the wrong way, not least villainous landlord Ray Mullan.

Emmerdale

But though some disapprove of
Cynthia's toughness, Danny's leisurely
way of approaching life – and Latisha's
propensity to steal anything not nailed
down – nobody can deny the Daggerts'
fierce determination to attain a better
life in Emmerdale.

Emmerdale

KATIE ADDYMAN
FIRST APPEARANCE: 2001
BORN: 1987

Katie is Andy's first girlfriend. They met in detention and have struggled to maintain their relationship in the face of their fathers' disapproval. Frustrated by being treated like children, Andy and Katie took the drastic step of getting deliberately pregnant. But though they may be rash and impulsive, nobody doubts their devotion to each other.

BRIAN ADDYMAN
FIRST APPEARANCE 2001
BORN: 1960

Katie's domineering father, Brian is the gardener at Home Farm. He has previously kept whippets.

Emmerdale

THE CALDER-WESTONS
FIRST APPEARANCE 2001

Phil Weston and Maggie Calder crashed simultaneously into the village and into each other's cars. Maggie, with her children Craig and Lucy had come to settle with Phil and daughter Jess to a new life in Emmerdale. From the outset, the makeshift family were plagued with problems.

Emmerdale

Nicola Blackstock made Maggie's life miserable and tried to break up the family. When it was discovered that Maggie had been sleeping with her boss, Dale Park co-owner Rodney Blackstock, the family fell apart and the Calders and Westons went their separate ways.

Emmerdale

SYD AND JERRY
FIRST APPEARANCE: 2002

Sydney Woolfe and Jerry "Mack" Mackinley arrived in Emmerdale to work on Viv Hope's cafe conversion, but before long Syd was trying to tear himself from the clinging clutches of Nicola Blackstock and Mack was getting in deep with Diane.

Emmerdale

RAY MULLAN
FIRST APPEARANCE: 2001
BORN: 1956

Club owner and building contractor Ray has left a mysterious career of crime behind him to start a new life in Emmerdale. Blissfully in love with glamorous barmaid Louise Appleton, and rapidly becoming the most powerful man in the village, Ray seems to live a charmed existence.

Emmerdale

But behind the suave Irish charm there hides a tortured soul and Ray's enslavement to his violent nature could spell trouble for him – and for anybody close to him.

Emmerdale

LOUISE APPLETON
FIRST APPEARANCE: 2001
BORN: 1968

Sharp and sexy, Louise was turning heads and hearts (particularly poor Terry's) as soon as she arrived as a temporary barmaid in the Woolpack. With a string of disastrous relationships in her wake, this sassy sheila caused a stir when she took up with sexagenarian smoothie Rodney Blackstock.

Emmerdale

Terry pined for her but Ray won her.
Now blissfully engaged and co-licensee
of the Woolpack, Louise seems on top of
the world. But how long can it last...?

Emmerdale

STEPH STOKES
FIRST APPEARANCE: 2002
BORN 1956

Steph arrived unexpectedly at Marlon and Tricia's engagement party and rashly thumped her future son-in-law. Tricia was shocked to see her estranged mother and Steph immediately made waves with her glamour and her mysterious shady past.

LAUREL POTTS
FIRST APPEARANCE: 2002
BORN: 1974

Hyperactive cleaner Laurel Potts also turned up at Marlon and Tricia's engagement. Less glamorous than Steph, she was dressed as a bumblebee and collapsed in agony with a burst appendix. She has since endeared herself to Betty and taken up lodgings with her and Seth.

Emmerdale

CLASSIC QUOTES

EMMERDALE may be known for some of its more dramatic storylines, but there is also some very funny dialogue to enjoy as well. Here is a tiny selection of some of the best.

Emmerdale

Biff: 'I can't propose to [Kathy] with a cake!'

Betty: 'Why not? It's dead romantic! I'd be on cloud nine if someone asked for my hand with the aid of a dedicated sponge.'

Betty on Diane: 'At the end of the day you're nowt but an over made-up trollop in a wig.'

Emmerdale

Betty on Rodney (post heart attack): 'He were as white as a sheet when they carried him out to the ambulance. Well – p'raps not a sheet. That tan of his'd take some shifting.'

Edna: 'Put this in your minutes: Mrs Birch was not happy.'

Diane: 'Put in the minutes?! It'll be your epitaph, that.'

Emmerdale

Edna (with reference to Turner's girth): 'I've sung more songs in that church than you've had hot dinners. Mind... it's probably a close call...'

Edna on Gloria: 'She's got more brass than a guesthouse gong.'

Emmerdale

Edna on Bob – Viv's first romantic encounter in ages: 'By 'eck, I hope he likes mothballs…'

Emmerdale

Viv: 'Of all the fish in the sea, my Bob is the rarest of catches – and there's none with a rod and line as particular as mine.'

Edna: 'No – nor as frequently cast.'

Emmerdale

Viv on gossip: 'I run the post office; it's my duty to inform.'

Emmerdale

Viv on Charity: 'Whoever heard of a bisexual prostitute coming between a lesbian millionairess and her wheelchair-bound brother? It's a wonder you're not on the front of every tabloid in the land.'

Viv on the supposedly dying Mrs Kirk: 'Look on the bright side. At least you won't have to worry about how to celebrate the Millennium.'

Emmerdale

Bernice (on Viv): She'll be making eyes at the undertaker when she's laying on the slab.'

Emmerdale

Bernice (on the importance of a good body): 'I see women eyeing me enviously every day over my Gavin. And that's *not* because of his brains or his personality.'

Tricia: 'Well I won't argue with that…'

Tricia: 'I'm not one to blow me own trumpet – am I Bernice?'

Bernice: 'No, I can truthfully say that I've never heard a single blast from it.'

Ray on Christmas in Emmerdale:
'If there are three wise men and
a virgin in this village then I
haven't seen them.'

Diane: '[Carlos] wants to know whose baby it is.'

Bernice: 'I hope you told him it was mine.'

Emmerdale

Emily: 'He kissed me.

Nicola: 'Were there tongues involved?'

Emily: 'He didn't *lick* me, he *kissed* me.'

Emmerdale

Marlon: 'Look the important thing to remember is that no matter what happens, you still have your dignity... Okay, maybe not your dignity but your will to live, right?'

Emmerdale

Sam: 'I had an imaginary friend once. But I didn't like him 'cause he was always picking on me...'

Zak's definition of happiness:
'My own drum kit and a woman
who welds.'

Emmerdale

Butch: 'What's Gomorrah, Dad?'

Zak: 'Don't worry son, you'll not catch it, clean living lad like you.'

Emmerdale

AMOS AND MR WILKS'S FINAL SCENE TOGETHER:

Amos: 'I think it's right going to a younger man.'

Henry: 'Ahh well, us old 'uns have got a few innings left in us yet hey?'

Amos: 'I certainly hope so, Henry.'

Henry: 'Henry... I can't remember the last time I heard you call me that.'

Amos: 'Well maybe it's not a night for formality, Mr Wilks.'

Emmerdale

Henry: 'Nay, nay, nay Mr Brearly, I think you're right.'

Amos: 'I shall miss it tha knows.'

Henry: 'Yes I know.'

Amos: 'Thee and all.'

Henry: 'Aye.'

Amos: 'Come here you silly old fool.'

They embrace.

Emmerdale

Marlon: 'Life ain't half a bag of poo!'